# Trade cash uncertainty for total cash confidence.

**Total Cash Confidence** comes from building an ever-evolving value creation system and focusing on the aspirations of your best clients and customers.

**Your Value-Creating KASH**

**Always Bigger, Better Bypass**

**Continually Improving Value**

**Right Place, Right Timing**

**Predictably Expansive**

**Profitably Accelerating Teamwork**

**Always More Useful**

**Can't Do It Wrong**

# Six Ways To Enjoy This Strategic Coach Book

| | |
|---|---|
| **Text**<br>**60 Minutes** | The length of our small books is based on the time in the air of a flight between Toronto and Chicago. Start reading as you take off and finish the book by the time you land. Just the right length for the 21st-century reader. |
| **Cartoons**<br>**30 Minutes** | You can also gain a complete overview of the ideas in this book by looking at the cartoons and reading the captions. We find the cartoons have made our Strategic Coach concepts accessible to readers as young as eight years old. |
| **Audio**<br>**120 Minutes** | The audio recording that accompanies this book is not just a recitation of the printed words but an in-depth commentary that expands each chapter's mindset into new dimensions. Download the audio at **strategiccoach.com/go/tcc** |
| **Video**<br>**30 Minutes** | Our video interviews about the concepts in the book deepen your understanding of the mindsets. If you combine text, cartoons, audio, and video, your understanding of the ideas will be 10x greater than you would gain from reading only. Watch the videos at **strategiccoach.com/go/tcc** |
| **Scorecard**<br>**10 Minutes** | Go to the Mindset Scorecard at the end of this book to score your Total Cash Confidence mindset. First, score yourself on where you are now, and then fill in where you want to be a year from now. Download additional copies at **strategiccoach.com/go/tcc** |
| **ebook**<br>**1 Minute** | After absorbing the fundamental ideas of the Total Cash Confidence concept, you can quickly and easily share them by sending the ebook version to as many other individuals as you desire. Direct them to **strategiccoach.com/go/tcc** |

# Thanks to the Creative Team:

Adam Morrison

Kerri Morrison

Hamish MacDonald

Shannon Waller

Jennifer Bhatthal

Victor Lam

Margaux Yiu

Christine Nishino

Willard Bond

Peggy Lam

Alex Varley

# Total Cash Confidence

Most entrepreneurs are fixated on their competition and on external conditions they can't control. To them, cash flow is a constant source of worry. What they don't realize is that their success *isn't actually about them at all.* It's about who they can create value for and what those people aspire to.

Entrepreneurs who know exactly how they create value can cross over a line where cash flow becomes certain, and the model they've created continually improves. Once you reach this point, you become totally confident that your cash flow will always be predictable—regardless of how the world outside your company changes.

Strategic Coach®, The Strategic Coach® Program, The Strategic Coach® Signature Program, Free Zone Frontier™, and The 10x Ambition Program™ are trademarks of The Strategic Coach Inc.

Cartoons by Hamish MacDonald.

Printed in Toronto, Canada. The Strategic Coach Inc., 33 Fraser Avenue, Suite 201, Toronto, Ontario, M6K 3J9.

This publication is meant to strengthen your common sense, not to substitute for it. It is also not a substitute for the advice of your doctor, lawyer, accountant, or any of your advisors, personal or professional.

If you would like further information about The Strategic Coach® Program or other Strategic Coach® services and products, please telephone 416.531.7399 or 1.800.387.3206.

Paperback ISBN: 978-1-64746-371-7
eBook ISBN: 978-1-64746-372-4
Library of Congress Control Number: 2020912641

# Contents

## Introduction

# Predictable And Enjoyable Money

You notice that while many entrepreneurs never get a confident handle on cash flow, you've made moneymaking increasingly predictable and enjoyable.

When you decided to be an entrepreneur, you took 100 percent responsibility for your own financial welfare, and this will never change. It's your way of life.

But if your way of making money as an entrepreneur is unpredictable and anxiety-inducing, then it's more like a life sentence.

The only way to do entrepreneurism well is to have total cash confidence. When you do, you'll free yourself from unpredictability and anxiety in your moneymaking.

### Never really sure.

There's something truly weird about the world of entrepreneurs: so much of what gets discussed is their constant uncertainty about future cash flow.

But the way you think about your own situation can be radically different.

You're an entrepreneur, and in the world of being an entrepreneur, there's no such thing as going too far into the area of being a unique individual. But you have to set up the conditions where you get rewarded for being a unique individual.

And you can't do that by comparing yourself to, and engaging in competition with, anyone else. It's impossible to operate uniquely if you're always comparing yourself to others and trying to compete with them.

Comparison and competition are a denial of individuality and uniqueness.

You can decide to embrace your uniqueness and individuality, and entirely avoid the game of competition and comparison that leads the vast majority of entrepreneurs to living their lives with uncertainty and anxiety about cash flow.

## They're anxious; you're not.
All of the anxious entrepreneurs out there simply don't seem to understand where all of the biggest and best cash flow comes from.

They think that cash confidence means having a certain amount of money. But there's no amount of money they can make that will get rid of their anxiety about cash flow.

You see, cash confidence isn't having an *amount* of money; it's a way of making money. It's a system you can adopt, and it means that you can focus on finding innovative solutions in the marketplace instead of just offering the same thing as everyone else and competing over price.

## Why you're so different.
Most entrepreneurs don't innovate at all. They take something someone else has created and try to outsell their competition. They usually attempt this by lowering their price, because that's the only way they can think of to set themselves apart.

11

But whereas these entrepreneurs think about money in terms of unpredictable, competitive products, services, and pricing, your approach to continually creating and expanding cash flow can be entirely different.

Your whole entrepreneurial relationship to money can be in a completely different universe—a universe of innovation and value creation.

## Deeper than the money.

The best entrepreneurs' value creation model is about who their best clients and customers are, what those people aspire to, and what the entrepreneur can do, along with other entrepreneurs, to help their clients and customers reach their goals.

With this approach, you become so confident about cash flow that you never have to worry about where it's going to come from in the future. You have an amazing entrepreneurial capability that's far more deeply and permanently secured than getting paid; you're forever freed up to focus on something far more important for your future success and growth.

You're going to be incredibly more successful and valuable to the best kind of customers and clients in the marketplace than you would be if you toiled anxiously in the traditional product- and service-selling competitive world.

You won't have to spend your time and energy in uncertainty about having enough cash flow, and you won't have to pay close attention to what other people are doing so that you can see how well you're doing in comparison with them.

There's a formula you'll use that will result in your continually getting bigger, better, and more valuable to the unique individuals you want to be a hero to.

## Sudden new understanding.
The cash flow system you've been developing and expanding for many years—in truth, actually, for your entire life—is simply the by-product of your 100 percent understanding of what it means to be an entrepreneur in the 21st century.

The more time, attention, and energy you spend thinking about your customers and clients—*what are their dangers, opportunities, and strengths? What are they trying to achieve in their world?*—the more value you're creating, and that gives you more cash confidence.

The big step is recognizing the only thing that matters: how other people see their future and how you can help them with that future. The more time you spend identifying and clarifying what your customers and clients want, and then helping them get it, the more your cash confidence grows.

Those who take this approach have a very different relationship with the marketplace than competitors do.

Entrepreneurs with total cash confidence have ever-expanding futures and reach new levels of collaborative teamwork.

It isn't about out-working or outsmarting anyone else; it's all about being smart in relationship to a unique and specific network of clients and customers who are also always getting smarter and whose visions of their futures are always getting bigger.

# Chapter 1
# Your Value-Creating KASH

You always focus on integrating your own unique knowledge, attitudes, skills, and habits into value creation that produces more money.

There's a concept called KASH, which stands for Knowledge, Attitudes, Skills, and Habits, that dates back to at least the 1950s. The idea behind it is that mastery of anything consists of four components.

*Knowledge* is the entirety of your experience and learning, and is always growing based on new experience and the acquisition of new information and facts. *Attitudes* are the way you think and feel about people and things. They're reflected in your behavior and emotional responses.

*Skills* are partly based on your natural abilities and partly based on your knowledge, experience, and practice of particular activities and tasks. *Habits* are the activities you do automatically and unconsciously. When an action is repeated regularly, it becomes habit.

All of these are interrelated. Your attitudes affect the knowledge you acquire, your skills are often based on your knowledge, your habits are repetitions of your skills, and so on.

These four attributes, when used to create unique value that others are willing to pay for, lead to having total cash confidence.

## Money is the by-product.
The key to increasing your cash confidence isn't to actually make more money but to create greater value for others. Making money is just the by-product of your value creation. People get fixated on calculating how much money they've made, but this is just a way of taking stock of your achievements and how you can surpass them. For me, money is a measurement of my achievements, but it's also a means for acquiring greater knowledge, attitudes, skills, and habits.

But you have to have time for all of that. Having total cash confidence continually buys you the time to be a greater value creator. Having the skill of total cash confidence makes all sorts of other things possible.

## Surprising new knowledge.
When your focus is always on value creation, you get to experience being surprised by new knowledge about the things at which you're masterful. Your own unique failures and successes enable you to gain new knowledge about how you can be valuable to those who will pay for it.

They'll pay you more as you get more masterful and will consider it worthwhile. Your knowledge will always be increasing, and the attitudes, skills, and habits will follow.

## Integrating and improving.
You can continually integrate your new value creation knowledge to improve your existing attitudes toward moneymaking opportunities.

No matter how much you know about creating value for your customers and clients, you always want to know more, and these value creation attitudes always create new moneymaking possibilities.

The more you know what constitutes value for your customers as they go forward in their lives, the more value you can create for them in the future relative to their aspirations. And then you can collaborate with others to multiply the value you're creating for those customers.

The freedoms you get from total cash confidence can be ten times more powerful in the future than they are right now, but it's not about making ten times the cash. It's about making the value creation ten times as great. Again, the money is just a by-product of that activity.

## Bypassing conventional rules.

Business books will tell you that you have to be totally aware of what your competitors are doing and price yourself accordingly. But in the total cash confidence model, pricing is strictly an agreement between you and the customer. It has nothing to do with what competitors are offering or what they're trying to solve because none of the fundamental information you need is coming from your competitors.

Rather, it's all coming from the ongoing conversations you have with your customers and clients in the marketplace. That's the only source of information that's really valuable to you. And because the value you create is unique, conventional rules don't apply to how you make money.

Here's an example of how this works: during the economic downturn in 2008, I asked a group of entrepreneurs how many of them would be okay for cash even if they didn't make money that quarter. I then shared the idea that they treat their best customers to a meal and never talk about themselves during that time—it had to be all about how the customer was doing, how they were approaching what was going on, and how they'd like to see themselves a year from now. One entrepreneur did this with 25 clients and reported back that it was the best quarter he'd ever had.

The reason this worked was because his clients had run out of future. There was no money for him when the quarter began because everybody's future had run out, and he was trying to sell something to people who didn't see a future. But with the investment of his time with 25 people, he created a mass amount of future. They didn't have any *present money* to spend, but they had all sorts of *future money* to spend once they saw a bigger future through their conversations with him.

Price competition is competing over present money, but value creation is creating future money, and we're always paid with future money.

## They don't have your KASH.

Your increasing knowledge, attitudes, skills, and habits for creating greater cash will enable you to completely ignore all competitors who don't know what you're doing. Your value creation KASH increasingly gives you total cash confidence.

The proof of total cash confidence is how much you and your company can be thinking about creating value for your customers and clients rather than thinking about yourselves and your business.

Indeed, with your value creation formula, you could lose everything you have, be plunked down in a new city, and recreate your income from scratch because you know how to create cash no matter the circumstances.

# WHAT IT ALL MEANS

**KNOWLEDGE**

YOU CONFIDENTLY UNDERSTAND AN ENTIRE SYSTEM OF CREATING VALUE THAT WILL ALWAYS PRODUCE BIGGER AND BETTER REVENUES AND PROFITS.

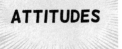

**ATTITUDES**

YOU ARE INCREASINGLY ALERT, CURIOUS, RESPONSIVE, AND RESOURCEFUL IN MAKING CRUCIAL IMPROVEMENTS WITHIN YOUR UNIQUE MONEYMAKING SYSTEM.

**SKILLS**

YOU HAVE COMPLETELY ORGANIZED ALL OF THE UNIQUE MONEYMAKING ABILITIES -- YOURS AND OTHERS' -- THAT CAN CONTINUALLY BE IMPROVED AND ADDED TO THE SYSTEM.

**HABITS**

YOU AND YOUR MONEYMAKING TEAM CONTINUALLY STRENGTHEN AND EXPAND ALL OF YOUR INTEGRATED KNOWLEDGE, ATTITUDES, AND SKILLS ON A PERMANENT DAILY BASIS.

# Chapter 2
## Always Bigger, Better Bypass
Your unique KASH formula always enables you to create bigger and better revenue and profit results from year to year.

Your greater understanding of the KASH system that underlies your total cash confidence will mean that you'll be constantly going out and finding more and more aspirational clients and customers for whom you can create greater value. The result of that will be more money showing up for you in both revenues and profits.

In my coaching career, I started off with a few individual clients whom I coached one on one, and once I reached about 50 clients, it was taking up all my time. We then switched over to a workshop format, where I could coach many individuals in one room on the same day, and we got up to about 500 clients.

Since then, we've introduced additional coaches and more workshops, and the number of current clients is about 2,500.

But no matter how much our group of clients may grow, it's still all about looking at value creation for individuals out in the marketplace.

### Unique knowledge formula.
When you have a continual formula for creating value based on your knowledge of your clients and customers, it sets you apart from everybody else. No one can copy you. No one can recreate what you do because no one else

is involved in the interchange you have with your clients and customers who are trying to create their own unique futures.

From the very start, everything about what you're doing is unique. It's based on your unique knowledge, attitudes, skills, and habits, all related to your unique clientele's unique aspirations.

## Always better measurements.
Inside any good system, there's some simple scorekeeping going on to make sure you're getting bigger and better results. But those results have to be bigger and better in the lives of your clients and customers before they become bigger and better in yours.

You need to have a growing system of unique principles, strategies, and measurements that enable you to create new and better value in ways that competitors can't see, and these unique measurements will create new ways of making the most money.

The more you help your customers and clients get bigger and better measurable results, the more value they'll see in working with you.

It's all related to what those individuals are looking for in the future and to your ability to help them measure their future results. If the results aren't defined by a number or event, then the human brain won't take it all that seriously, and there won't be a definitive way of measuring success.

It's important to understand that these measurements of success are unique. You're not learning these measurements from the outside world. You're not learning them from people who are competing with you. They're all within the mind of the individual you want to create value for.

## Profitably improving revenues.

It's important to always be increasing what works and eliminating what doesn't in your value creation process so that each new improvement will automatically make your system more profitable.

The things that work keep eliminating everything that isn't profitable. Your good habits crowd out your bad ones.

If you're charging a certain amount and making a certain amount of profit on what you're charging, and then you try to raise the price, you'll probably be met with resistance.

But if you vastly increase your value creation, the new money is going to come to you a lot more easily. Every time your value creation jumps up a level, so does your profitability. Profitability is geared to value creation.

As you constantly update your value creation process based on what works and what doesn't, you're always keeping in mind that it isn't about you—it's what works and what doesn't work in creating value for your clients and customers.

## Always bigger than before.

When you continually explore more deeply and decisively inside of your uniquely integrated process of more valuable knowledge, attitudes, skills, and habits, it keeps becoming more fascinating and motivating to you.

You'll be rewarded psychologically, emotionally, and cre- atively as you make this process work better and better. It's emotion-driven rather than simply focused on numbers or measurements. The actual activity will be fulfilling.

The way to check if it's really working is to look at whether it's creating greater value for your clients and customers.

From the outside, no one can see exactly what it is you're doing, but you know there are others who are taking the same approach, doing this in their own unique way.

## Bypassing other people's standards.

Your unique moneymaking system neither compares nor competes with how others are trying to make money because their best practices are all about making more money, while your KASH process is all about creating greater value. You are completely differentiated from anyone else so there's no experience of competition.

It comes back to the idea that money is a by-product and a measurement of your value creation. Money provides electricity for the system, and you know how to always keep it flowing.

If money, the by-product, ever becomes your goal, you lose all sense of how it's actually being created, what the actual source is for making money. If making money is your goal, then everything is all about you rather than about creating value for your customers and clients.

Your focus must always be on creating value and improving your value creation system. The most successful entrepreneurs are those who are always creating new kinds of value that far surpass their industry.

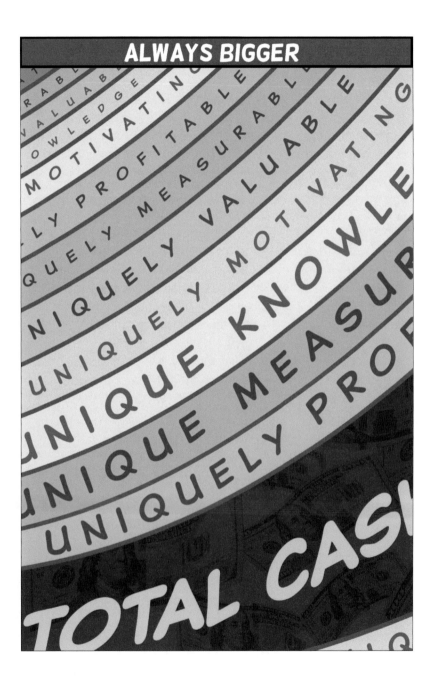

# Chapter 3
## Continually Improving Value

Your confidence about growing your financial results enables you to focus more of your time on improving the value you create for your clientele.

It's all about being freed up from focusing on moneymaking so you can devote your time and attention to creating greater value for your customers and clients. And the more time and attention you devote to creating greater value, the more your money's guaranteed.

What happens is that your clients and customers become part of your innovation team. Instead of spending hours and hours by yourself trying to come up with a solution, you spend more time finding out from them what the solution would look like.

So you're not a servant in the marketplace; it's a partnership where you're the *creative partner* and your customers and clients are the *aspirational partners*. What they bring to the table are their bigger and better goals, and instead of just approaching you and requesting a solution, they're collaborators with you in the creative process.

### More capable and confident.

Even though you're confident in your own unique KASH system, you'll want to go outside of yourself so you can start adding other people's knowledge, attitudes, skills, and habits to your value creation process. You want to build a value creation team

You're looking for people whose knowledge and experience are totally different from yours, who will have different attitudes than yours—though still positive attitudes—and who will bring in different skills and habits than those you provide.

Organizations that are "cash anxious" or "cash uncertain" tend to be understaffed because they see hiring people as a real risk. They hear that other businesses are laying off employees, so they think they should too. But they're basing the decision on second- or third-hand information about what's going to happen in the marketplace.

That's gossip, and it has nothing to do with how money is actually generated.

But if, every quarter, you can see how you can be freed up more to be in the value creation mode, you'll recognize who you need to hire to handle certain parts of what you're doing. Your role as the entrepreneur is to see where your use of time could be enhanced if you hired the right people.

The way you develop and expand your unique value in the marketplace is through a teamwork process that's entirely self-created, and this means that your personal and organizational confidence is self-generating, as is your capability for future growth.

### Observable "competitive" success.
To outside observers, it's going to look like you're extremely competitive. But the truth is that inside of your financial planning and implementation, you're paying no attention at all to what any of your so-called competitors are doing.

What you're doing is always creating new solutions that are completely competition-free.

onventional "experts."

ts" in the competitive marketplace will claim
you're succeeding, you can always have
the com..... t certainty that you're achieving entirely new
kinds of breakthroughs. This is because your value creation
breakthrough can only be understood by doing it. All mastery is in the specifics, not in generalities.

Your first-class value creation comes from an enormous
number of unique specifics that you're putting together.
And unless someone is inside the unique value creation
process and knows why each part of it was created, how
it continues to get better, and how it's all triggered by your
unique relationship with your aspirational partners, they
don't really understand what's going on. That applies both
to would-be competitors and to marketplace experts.

The experts don't want you to be unique; they want you to
be conforming.

## Transforming clients' freedom.

But you have a secret for always making more money in
the marketplace, and it's simply this: while everyone else
is increasingly trying to copy the competition, all of your
attention and creativity is focused on transforming the
freedom capabilities of your very best clientele.

You're always freeing yourself up to free up others.

Freedom capabilities are defined by the four freedoms
of time, money, relationship, and purpose. With all value
creation, the person you're creating value for experiences
greater freedom than before they started working with you.
Their time is freer, there's no limit to the amount of money
they can make, their most important relationships improve,

and their purpose grows. And as with everything in this system, the way they define their purpose is unique in terms of their specifics.

Thinking about their customers and clients and not themselves requires a huge mindset shift for some people because of how they've been brought up and trained. But a good way to reinforce this mindset and determine whether you're creating value is to ask yourself if what you're doing is expanding the other person's freedom capabilities.

If it can't be measured in terms of improving those four freedoms, it's lacking in value creation.

## Self-generating moneymaker.
Your increasing commitment and courage to create a self-generating moneymaking process means that how you create new value for your bigger and better clients is also self-generating.

Your aspirational customers and clients want greater freedom, and if you continually help them achieve it in the four ways we measure it, that will automatically generate more money for you.

Remember that every client is a market of one. You can learn from each market, and you have skills that are useful in all markets, but each client's aspirations are unique, and what you do for them is unique.

Your attention and focus are on deepening and expanding something that represents an entirely independent market.

# Chapter 4
# Right Place, Right Timing

Your greater focus on creating unique value — superior to the conventional offerings of any competitors — enables you to always be ready for the next best opportunity.

The vast majority of entrepreneurs have a lot more to think about than you do because they don't have cash flow confidence. So when a new opportunity comes up, they're very slow in reacting or they don't even see the opportunity at all.

This is because their thinking is in the past. They're concerned about things they didn't do that have put them in their current situation of uncertain cash flow.

But if you're an entrepreneur with cash confidence, you're always living entirely in the present and watching for new opportunities that come along. Everything in the past has already been handled. You and your company are always right up to date.

## Always greater attention.

Since you have an increasing personal and organizational mastery of your autonomous value creation system, you're able to focus your best attention on new areas of money-making.

You're always ready to take on the best, newest opportunity. You have total cash confidence, and so does your company. And because you're not competing, you're creating new value.

You're not trying to match what everyone else is doing. You're simply taking what you've already created and extending it further into new territory.

If your value creation weren't set in a system and process, you wouldn't know how to keep improving what you're doing. But you're not dealing with a series of one-offs. You're always solidifying and what you already have. And all that value creation you do results in profitable money-making.

## Permanently ahead.
Having this self-generating value creation and moneymaking system puts you permanently ahead of every other development taking place in your market and industry.

New developments in industries are always the average result of what everybody is doing. When you go to an industry meeting, there are no breakthroughs; there are just better examples of best practices.

These are people who aren't actually doing anything new. They're hitting more of the right notes, but everybody knows what the notes are. But you're playing a different tune. You're creating new musical instruments.

You don't care what everybody else knows. You care only about what you and your clients know. So, your path of continuous innovation is a forward-moving relationship with your clients, not a sideways-moving relationship with your industry.

Your way of always moving ahead is by reducing the attention on yourself and your company to the bare minimum, and focusing on the goals and challenges of your customers and clients. This enables you to give full attention to what's possible outside of yourself and your company.

## Best emerging aspirations.

Every day, you can focus your attention on what's happening next for your clientele. You don't need to concern yourself with anything except the emerging growth goals of your best customers and clients who are your aspirational partners.

Each of their situations includes specific dangers to overcome, opportunities to capture, and strengths to reinforce. Because you're cash confident, you're able to ignore everything else so that you're as alert as possible for them.

## Always ready to respond.

Those with cash confidence always put themselves in the best possible position to respond to entirely new challenges and requirements for higher level performance and achievements.

You have capabilities, your customers and clients have challenges, and you're putting your maximum capabilities together with their most unique emerging challenges.

Anyone who tries to compete with you is reacting to you, not to their own opportunities. But your value creation system is unique, and so is the relationship you have with your clients and customers, so what you're doing simply can't be copied.

Those entrepreneurs who are trying to do what everyone else is doing aren't available, as you are, for the biggest and best opportunities for value creation that arise.

## Next best opportunities.

While so many others are always looking back, living in the past, you're always moving on from what you've already accomplished.

Your complete system of transformative knowledge, attitudes, skills, and habits is always up to date, and this enables you to take advantage of your next best opportunities. You're always right here, in the present.

At the end of each day, you ask, "What's new for tomorrow?" And you're not focused on what's new for you and your company, but rather what's new for your clients and customers.

It takes a lot of coordinated muscles to do this. The knowledge, attitudes, skills, and habits are all part of your system, and you're always gaining more and more knowledge about how the system works. The KASH system is meaningless if it doesn't make money, just as cash itself is meaningless if it's not supported by a KASH system.

If there are any glitches, friction, or bumps in the system, you're constantly smoothing them out. You have attitudes about how to apply your knowledge and whom you apply it to that are all geared toward understanding the minds of your clients—and you're always making sure that the clients you're working with meet your criteria of being aspirational partners.

# Chapter 5
## Predictably Expansive
Your improved alertness and responsiveness always make each year's greater moneymaking a sure thing.

A lot of people think that if you're an entrepreneur, you can never be certain that your income will increase from one year to the next.

And I wonder, who'd want to live like that?

It's true that all entrepreneurs have taken a risk by deciding that they're responsible for their own financial welfare, but it's only some entrepreneurs who live in the worst of both worlds, having both no security *and* no certainty.

These are the entrepreneurs who think only about themselves and how they're doing in comparison with other entrepreneurs.

The ones who make it a goal to free themselves up as much as possible to focus on the aspirations of their customers and clients find security in opportunity. These entrepreneurs can be sure they'll make more money from year to year.

As a cash confident entrepreneur, rather than think about how you're doing, you think about how useful you're being to people who can write you big checks.

## Responding to clientele aspirations.

You want all of your clients to be aspirational partners. Aspirational partners will keep writing you bigger and bigger checks for helping them achieve their bigger and bigger goals.

That's what continually multiplies your revenues and profits: your single focus on the unique aspirations of your best clientele.

Your best clients and customers are after the same thing as everybody else, which is greater freedoms in the categories of time, money, relationship, and purpose—but with their own specificities unique to them.

More than anyone else, you can be the person your clients share their aspirations with, with the result that you know more than anyone about their futures and what drives them. Other people in their lives don't necessarily wish them freedom, but you do, and you're their creative partner when it comes to their achievements and growth.

## Bypassing competitors' activities.

In your work of continually transforming your clients' freedom aspirations into new, innovative solutions, you're always pioneering entirely new territory that no one else even knows exists.

As a result, you can permanently ignore and bypass the commoditizing activities of every kind of would-be competitor.

It can seem like your industry is a mighty entity, but it's really just the existing average of the mediocrity of all the people who think they're competing with you.

There's no value creation material there unless you teach them. But who would you rather improve: a great aspirational partner and client, or a mediocre competitor?

Every industry is commoditized. It's not an industry unless everyone's doing the same thing, and it's all based on price competition.

But in your world, pricing is a function of how innovative you are and how big your clients' aspirations are.

## Predictably more money.

Always creating bigger and better innovative solutions for your clientele will predictably generate more money for you regardless of changes in the economy or marketplace.

The only things that change for you are your clients' bigger aspirations and your innovative solutions. You're in a zone by yourself because what you do is strictly a relationship between your innovation and other people's aspiration. It has nothing to do with anything else going on.

Even in situations where everyone else is slowing down because of some outside factor, you might find it's an environment for opportunity because all that matters is between you and your clients.

## Always more than enough.

Your predictably expanding innovation always produces more solutions, and these solutions always earn you more than enough money to be even more innovatively useful.

As your aspirational partnerships deepen and expand, money is an automatic by-product. It's constant growth.

Your clients' aspirations get bigger, you come up with bigger innovative solutions, and more money comes your way.

You'll find that you have to reject some people as clients because your growing capabilities always have to be freed up to match the highest aspiration.

What keeps me feeling younger now, at 75, than I did before is gearing myself up to improve my capabilities to meet the challenges faced by my biggest aspirational partners. They're always getting better, I'm always getting better, the results are always getting better, and the money's always getting better.

Tell me what's not to like about that!

## Continually more certain.

As long as you're committed to creating even greater value, this closed-loop system of aspiration focus, innovative solutions, and greater profitability means you can be totally certain about moneymaking.

As uncertainty is always increasing for competitors, your money is always becoming more predictably certain.

There's no award ceremony for doing this. The work, the activity itself, is the reward and the recognition. You'll always find that yesterday was a good day, and today is better.

As you expand your KASH system, your cash flow remains a certainty, and you'll be able to always move forward with confidence to bigger and better activities. You know that as opportunities come up, you'll always be in a position to respond to them immediately and effectively.

# Chapter 6
# Profitably Accelerating Teamwork
Your predictable cash-growing system enables you to continually attract individuals whose superior teamwork skills free you up.

In every situation, once I've handled my part of a teamwork project, I stop thinking about it because I know that the other people on the team will handle their parts of the job.

It's not that I don't believe they have their own challenges; it's just that I know that they're on top of what they do and I trust them to do it. They know I'll get my part done, and when the ball is in their court, I don't spend any time at all thinking about it because I'm confident it will get handled.

The only checklist I need to go over in my head is who's on the team.

As you push for higher value creation, there will be more and more that has to be completely handled by others. It's crucial to build a team around you that you trust.

## Faster growing cash system.
Other skilled value creators on your team will continually free you up to innovate at a higher level. This means that your moneymaking confidence, and everyone else's, will grow at a faster rate.

Your own better value creation always triggers bigger cash flow. Your collaborators are seeing your aspirations and creating new systems and new methods to support them.

It's all about teamwork. This isn't a one-person operation.

When it comes to how many people you need working on a project, the answer is that the team is always as big as it has to be for the level of value creation you're aiming for and to meet the level of the aspirational clients.

## Attracting skilled moneymakers.

You'll never have to worry about finding the right people to collaborate with you, because you and your cash-confident system will be a magnet for other talented and committed players.

Your organization's unique, innovative reputation in the marketplace will be enough to attract like-minded individuals, and those individuals' own value creation skills will quickly generate greater revenues and profits.

These types of desirable collaborators out there, and they're looking for an organization that's continually innovating and constantly onto bigger and better things. The ongoing nature of this means that you'll always be attracting new and better people to collaborate with you.

And because every collaborator has a distinct role, and no one's worried or otherwise thinking about how everyone else is doing their job, there's no competition, which means the project is completely free of politics and no energy goes into positioning.

## Superior teamwork liberates.

Your approach to business, value creation, and moneymaking liberates everyone on your growing team from the adversarial negativity and limitations of scarcity and competition.

Your focus on always greater freedom for everyone is contagious. Freedom is the yardstick for measuring success. It's what everyone is looking for in their lives.

While most entrepreneurs spend an enormous amount of time and energy on the useless activity of comparing themselves to others, everyone on your team is focusing on what they do best and on expanding that uniqueness.

This means that each of you will have a lot more free time and energy to grow your capabilities and to create greater value for your customers and clients.

## Always more motivated.

As your measurable results of both unique value creation and moneymaking increase on a predictable growth curve, you'll find that everyone in your system—especially your aspirational clientele—feels increasingly motivated to gain even more.

Your growing mastery of cash confidence will be extraordinarily compelling for everyone who encounters you.

And you're going to want to eliminate from your system every individual who isn't motivated and aspirational. That includes both the people inside your company and the clients and customers you create value for.

There might be a lot of unmotivated and non-aspirational people in the world, but as long as you're not involved with them, it doesn't matter. They won't interfere with what you're doing.

You only want to collaborate with individuals who are operating at a high level.

## Freedom from retirement.

Because of their endless cash uncertainties, people who compete always have retirement in mind as their endgame. These competitors are striving to generate a surplus of cash so that they can stop competing and have enough money to get by.

But that's completely gone from your future. Cash confidence, you'll find, is both its own reward and its own new starting point.

Why would you want to retire when you have a system in place so that you never have to worry about cash flow or competition, and you're continually getting bigger and better and being challenged by other people's bigger and better aspirations?

No longer doing that wouldn't be a reward.

You're always being useful and on your way to becoming more useful. Retirement would mean that you're being taken out of use.

People for whom money is the goal, who measure success by particular markers of lifestyle, aim to retire once they reach a certain point. But if what you do never becomes boring, and money for you just is a by-product of what you do, you'll never want to stop.

# Chapter 7
## Always More Useful

You notice as you increasingly grow — while commoditized competitors slow, stop, and fail — that you have a secret formula that works.

Competition is geared toward price. So if you're competing, you have to always be very alert to anybody else trying to sell the commodity you're selling because, at least in the points of view of customers and clients, all of you are selling the same thing.

You might want to differentiate yourself, but since the customers only see you selling the same product as other people, the only benefit you can offer that will really interest them is a lower price.

With a total cash confidence system, however, you might be in the same industry as a lot of other people, but your clients and customers see you as unique. This is because you don't package what you sell in terms of price, but in terms of the specific clients' unique aspirations.

Through their aspirations, you're uniquely connected to the customers and clients themselves.

### Expert on biggest aspirations.
Because you have an expanding understanding of other people's biggest aspirations and how they can best be achieved, you can provide them with increasingly innovative strategies and structures.

The best individuals with the biggest visions will seek you out as an expert on how to move forward.

At the same time, you're also an expert on recognizing which individuals have big aspirations and which don't, which is important because you want to match your capabilities with the biggest aspirations out there.

I prefer working with people who have really big ambitions, who have no deadline for stopping what they're doing, and who are always exploring new territory that requires skills, capabilities, and resources they don't already have.

As a cash-confident entrepreneur who's always improving your KASH, you stay alert, curious, responsive, and resourceful about your clients' unique aspirations, which are continually changing as their thoughts about their futures change in response to what's going on in the world. You stay up to date and pay attention as much as possible.

Your clients stick with you because they're betting that you'll continue to be at the top of your game, helping to keep them at the top of their game.

## Making it up, making it real.

Being a great aspiration and achievement guide for others means that you grow two capabilities: helping others to clarify their vision, and then helping them to see exactly how to achieve it. You grasp what it is they want, and then you provide the capabilities for them to get it.

Your clients and customers will always keep you on your toes with their evolving aspirations. Every time they're ready to take a leap, you have to fully understand what they're going for, and then think up the best way for them to achieve their goals.

You have to innovate with tools, techniques, processes, and structures to allow them to take their aspirations and achieve new things that are bigger and better than anything they've done before.

## Bypassing all comparison.

In the past, you devoted your time and energy to thinking about measuring up to the competition, but this is no longer the case. There's no longer any outside measurement for the innovative value you supply to your aspirational partners.

Competing is looking sideways. But looking at your clients is looking ahead.

About 15 years ago, I was asked if I had any problem with the fact that I don't have credentials or certification for being a coach. I said no, and that I'd never even thought about that. You can only certify the professions where the aspirations of the consumers are known and fixed.

The best clients, the ones who are aspirational partners, are constantly creating new territory that isn't covered by any existing method or tool. It's impossible to even know in advance what those areas are. And if these are the types of clients you work with, you're an entrepreneur who's operating 100 percent competition-free.

## Endlessly more valuable.

In the past, a significant part of your value was measured by how your price compared with competitors', but now your value is measured in terms of how you keep innovating new solutions for your best clientele's biggest aspirations.

This puts the issue of pricing in its proper place—that how much people will pay for something has nothing to do with what's reasonable from an outside observation. It has to do with what's being offered in relation to where they want to go.

It's hard for other people to wrap their minds around it in some cases, but if someone's happy to pay $1 million for something, that something is probably worth $10 million to them if it gets them to where they aspire to go.

There's no way to objectively determine what something's worth unless it's imposed from the outside. And between you and your clients, there's no such imposition. So, you keep becoming more valuable, with no reason to ever stop.

## Freedom from status.

You have jumped from the world where everybody's striving for higher status to your own self-transforming world of higher value creation.

Status is where you're rewarded for the level you've reached, and you don't have to be smart or creative anymore. The reward becomes automated, and because you've reached that level, you're guaranteed for life.

The best entrepreneurs aren't aiming for status, but rather striving to create greater and greater value for clients. And in that world, you'll never reach the point where you'll say you have enough and want to stop.

You're worth whatever your value is today, and your value is always increasing.

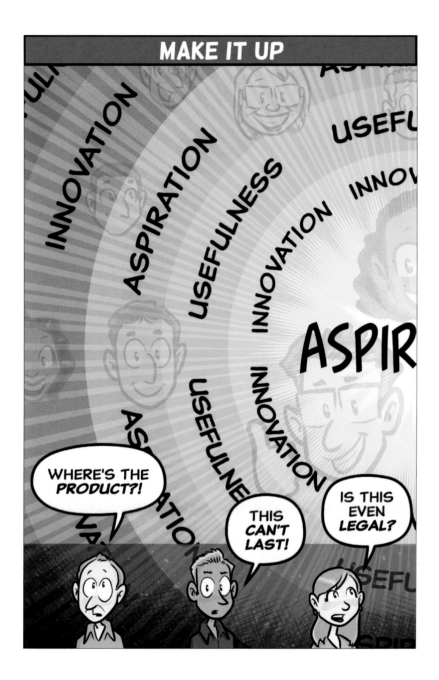

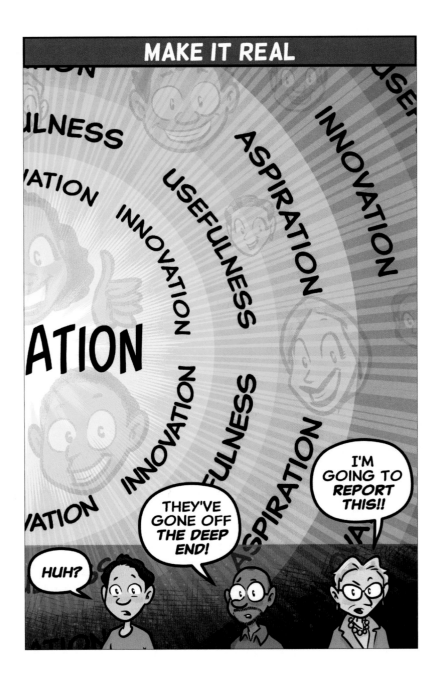

# Chapter 8
## Can't Do It Wrong

You and your team have improved and expanded your value creation so consistently that it's practically impossible to get anything wrong for very long.

You've based your reputation, skills, capabilities, success, and company purely on the attention you give to your unique customers and clients' aspirations, and there's no one who can compete with you in this realm.

Because of your connection with your clients and your proven record of working with these aspirational partners, they're not going to decide to go with someone else who'll do it for less. *No one else is choosing to do what you do at all.* There might be other people who have your level of skills, but they don't want to base their futures on clients' aspirations. They'd consider that a scary prospect.

Because all of their entrepreneurial education and experience, and all of their industry training about their products and services, is based on what everyone else is doing, they're just looking sideways at the competition, not looking ahead.

For you, the standard way of doing things leads to a painful, unsatisfying way of living as an entrepreneur. But your satisfying, innovative way of doing things just isn't an idea that would ever occur to most people.

## Consistently smarter teamwork.

The unique experience and value you provide to your clientele relates to your own individual skills, but as you go along, there have to be layers of teamwork for you to provide that value consistently and to add new features.

The collaborators you're looking for wouldn't want to work for someone who competes, but your focus on creating value makes you extraordinarily attractive to skilled individuals who want to contribute their capabilities to your value creation system.

More and more, your personal confidence becomes teamwork confidence.

Even if you started out as a solitary entrepreneur, it doesn't necessarily mean you're hardwired that way. As you build a team around you, you'll recognize your team members' unique capabilities and mastery of skills, and have faith that your level of value creation will continue even when you're not doing all the work yourself.

Moreover, because your team members will have skills and capabilities you don't have, the teamwork will result in extra dimensions of value you couldn't provide on your own.

## Alert, curious, responsive, resourceful.

Everything in your growing teamwork is characterized by increasing alertness, curiosity, responsiveness, and resourcefulness. Everything is alive, evolving, and energizing.

But to everyone on the outside looking in, it's a complete mystery what drives it. They'll come up with theories about how you get it done, but they'll bear no resemblance to what you're actually doing.

No outside observer can describe an organization with total cash confidence that's entirely generated by being alert, curious, responsive, and resourceful to the changing and challenging aspirations of its clientele.

There's no industry standard, or best practice, for that.

It's constantly being created uniquely by each entrepreneur who's doing it in relationship to their unique customers and clients.

## Never wrong for very long.
You and your team are continually in touch with the biggest and best aspirations of your clientele, and you're amazingly quick to adjust to any of their changes.

You're no longer going to make mistakes or experience failures that set you back or get you off track. You're in a permanent state of research and development, and you don't get too far ahead of yourself. You don't try to anticipate someone's needs before they experience them.

The only meaningful thing is the specific relationships you have with customers and clients. Every one of those relationships is a unique market and industry in and of itself.

You might sometimes get things wrong in the sense that you don't have them quite right, but you're always in the process of getting closer to right.

## Failures are breakthroughs.
You no longer experience failures in ways that are big, bad, or permanent. You'll notice failures the moment they happen, and just as quickly, you'll use them.

And you'll use them not only to make corrections, but to create entirely new breakthroughs. Everything you encounter is raw material for new, better innovations.

You won't fall in love with your ideas, at least until others have fallen in love with them, and even then you'll recognize that what's good for today might have to get a lot better soon.

You're always operating in a sort of testing ground where everything's being challenged, so you'll always be able to transform what you experience into something useful.

## Unique value, always expanding.

You no longer feel that unpredictably competitive things are happening to you, but rather that you and your value creation team are always the active, creative, innovative force in the world.

Uniquely valuable new solutions are always being created, and their impact is always expanding.

Within the framework of the unique relationships you've created with your aspirational customers, you're the best there is. There's no competition for that. And because the aspirations of your clientele are always growing and expanding, there's no limit when it comes to your future.

Since there's a strong connection between your unique capabilities and your clients' unique aspirations, you don't have to worry about the future—you're *creating* it.

# Conclusion
## Unique KASH Multiplies Cash

You are now set for life with an ever-improving system of increasing knowledge, attitudes, skills, and habits that generates ever-increasing amounts of aspirational money.

Like all the best systems, what you have with your KASH is a closed-loop system. The end of the process leads into the next level jump, where the process starts again.

And it's a learning system. If you're alert, curious, responsive, and resourceful, then you're always learning. So even though you're covering the same ground over and over again in the system, with each revolution you have more knowledge, a higher level of capability, and a new perspective.

What you're offering to clients is unique, and the more you go through your process, the bigger the checks the right clients will be happy to write.

### Set for your life ahead.

This system that you create from your own unique knowledge, attitudes, skills, and habits sets you free from all the anxious uncertainty that comes from competing over price with commoditized products and services that everyone else is trying to copy and steal.

You're now set for a unique moneymaking future that's entirely of your own design.

It's a misconception that marketplaces are created by entrepreneurs or corporations. They're created by people who are willing to pay more for something bigger, better, and different than they ever had before.

What you're doing is offering something that no one else can to people who will be excited to pay for it, because you're creating value that matches their own aspirations.

## Self-evolving system.

Unlike all of the anxious competitors outside of your system, you're at the center of how the biggest and best money will always be created in the world.

You can now spend all of your creative time, attention, and talent on growing something extraordinary that was always yours from the beginning. It's self-generating and self-contained. That doesn't mean that outside resources don't get added to it, but what really propels it are the relationships you have.

It's all based on those markets of one. And there are millions of them. These millions of unique economies actually push forward the big economy, though no one outside can measure them or compare with them.

## Creating its own expansion.

As your clients' aspirations are always increasing, so are your value creation, teamwork, collaboration, reputation, and referrals.

Your business of focusing on value creation is entirely different from focusing on competition. Once you take the risk of ignoring the competition, you create a unique economy that goes on for as long as you want to keep it going.

The best kind of money in the world reproduces itself in ever-larger amounts, because every bit of it is entirely based on aspiration, innovation, and value creation. And it's very satisfying money to make since it comes from your own unique innovation, creativity, and teamwork to support the aspirations of the clients you really want to be a hero to.

Your moneymaking system follows its own unique rules, and only you have the inside knowledge of what these are and how they work.

## Endlessly abundant collaboration.
You're always going to be as financially independent as you want to be, and at the same time, you're always going to be discovering and collaborating with other innovative value creators who are enjoyably expanding their own aspirational moneymaking systems.

None of these other innovators will have the slightest interest in competing with you because, in a world of growing cash abundance, there's no need to even think about competing.

The status and competition game is over. You and the other innovators you collaborate with don't need to be admired by competitors. You have to be clear about whom you want to notice you, and who's important to have in your future.

I want team members who understand the purpose of our company and whom we're creating value for, and I want them to be alert, curious, responsive, and resourceful to the people they need to be attentive to.

If there are entrepreneurs who are playing a different game than the creative, aspirational one we're playing, then we don't work together. We attract people who multiply our message out in the marketplace, and then we attract great collaborators—other entrepreneurs who are doing similar activities out in their own worlds.

We share tips and knowledge because we're not competing; we have similar goals.

## Seems like a miracle.
You can now see that what would look like a miraculous moneymaking system to outsiders—completely mysterious to their way of thinking and operating—is the only way to be totally cash confident.

Once you cross the line into this state of confidence, expecting and experiencing "money miracles" seems like the normal thing.

Competitors see cash confidence as *having* a certain amount of money, but creative collaborators know it's a way of *making* money. There's a world of difference between the two. One is in black and white, and one is in a full spectrum of color.

And as a matter of fact, I've never seen any amount of money give competitive people cash confidence.

When you connect your knowledge, attitudes, skills, and habits with the value you create for aspirational customers and clients, you achieve total cash confidence.

The Strategic Coach Program
## For Ambitious, Collaborative Entrepreneurs
You commit to growing upward through three transformative levels, giving yourself 25 years to exponentially improve every aspect of your work and life.

"Total Cash Confidence" is a crucial capability and a natural result of everything we coach in The Strategic Coach Program, a quarterly workshop experience for successful entrepreneurs who are committed and devoted to business and industry transformation for the long-term, for 25 years and beyond.

The Program has a destination for all participants—creating more and more of what we call "Free Zone Frontiers." This means taking advantage of your own unique capabilities, the unique capabilities around you, your unique opportunities, and your unique circumstances, and putting the emphasis on creating a life that is free of competition.

Most entrepreneurs grow up in a system where they think competition is the name of the game. The general way of looking at the world is that the natural state of affairs is competition, and collaboration is an anomaly.

### Free Zone Frontier
The Free Zone Frontier is a whole new level of entrepreneurship that many people don't even know is possible. But once you start putting the framework in place, new

possibilities open up for you. You create zones that are purely about collaboration. You start recognizing that collaboration is the natural state, and competition is the anomaly. It makes you look at things totally differently.

Strategic Coach has continually created concepts and thinking tools that allow entrepreneurs to more and more see their future in terms of Free Zones that have no competition.

### Three levels of entrepreneurial growth.
Strategic Coach participants continually transform how they think, make decisions, communicate, and take action based on their use of dozens of unique entrepreneurial mindsets we've developed. The Program has been refined through decades of entrepreneurial testing and is the most concentrated, massive discovery process in the world created solely for transformative entrepreneurs who want to create new Free Zones.

Over the years, we've observed that our clients' development happens in levels of mastery. And so, we've organized the Program into three levels of participation, each of which involves two different types of transformation:

**The Signature Level.** The first level is devoted to your *personal* transformation, which has to do with how you're spending your time as an entrepreneur as well as how you're taking advantage of your personal freedom outside of business that your entrepreneurial success affords you. Focusing on improving yourself on a personal level before you move on to making significant changes in other aspects of your life and business is key because you have to simplify before you can multiply.

The second aspect of the Signature Level is how you look at your *teamwork*. This means seeing that your future consists of teamwork with others whose unique capabilities complement your own, leading to bigger and better goals that constantly get achieved at a measurably higher rate.

**The 10x Ambition Level.** Once you feel confident about your own personal transformation and have access to ever-expanding teamwork, you can think much bigger in terms of your *company*. An idea that at one time would have seemed scary and even impossible—growing your business 10x—is no longer a wild dream but a result of the systematic expansion of the teamwork model you've established. And because you're stable in the center, you won't get thrown off balance by exponential growth. Your life stays balanced and integrated even as things grow around you.

And that's when you're in a position to transform your relationship with your *market*. This is when your company has a huge impact on the marketplace that competitors can't even understand because they're not going through this transformative structure or thinking in terms of 25 years as you are. Thinking in terms of 25 years gives you an expansive sense of freedom and the ability to have big picture goals.

**The Free Zone Frontier Level.** Once you've mastered the first four areas of transformation, you're at the point where your company is self-managing and self-multiplying, which means that your time can now be totally freed up. At this stage, competitors become collaborators and it becomes all about your *industry*. You can consider everything you've created as a single capability you can now match up with another company's to create collaborations that go way beyond 10x.

And, finally, it becomes *global*. You immediately see that there are possibilities of going global—it's just a matter of combining your capabilities with those of others to create something exponentially bigger than you could ever have achieved on your own.

## Global collaborative community.

Entrepreneurism can be a lonely activity. You have goals that the people you grew up with don't understand. Your family might not comprehend you at all and don't know why you keep wanting to expand, why you want to take new risks, why you want to jump to the next level. And so it becomes proportionately more important as you gain your own individual mastery that you're in a community of thousands of individuals who are on exactly the same journey.

In The Strategic Coach Program, you benefit from not only your own continual individual mastery but from the constant expansion of support from and collaboration with a growing global community of extraordinarily liberated entrepreneurs who will increasingly share with you their deep wisdom and creative breakthroughs as innovators in hundreds of different industries and markets.

If you've reached a jumping off point in your entrepreneurial career where you're beyond ready to multiply all of your capabilities and opportunities into a 10x more creative and productive formula that keeps getting simpler and more satisfying, we're ready for you.

**For more information and to register for The Strategic Coach Program, call 416.531.7399 or 1.800.387.3206, or visit us online at *strategiccoach.com*.**

## THREE LEVELS OF
# FREE ZONE FRONTIER

| | | | |
|---|---|---|---|
| 25 | 26 | 27 | 28 |
| 29 | 30 | 31 | 32 |
| 33 | 34 | 35 | 36 |

# 10X AMBITION

| | | | |
|---|---|---|---|
| 13 | 14 | 15 | 16 |
| 17 | 18 | 19 | 20 |
| 21 | 22 | 23 | 24 |

# SIGNATURE

| | | | |
|---|---|---|---|
| 1 | 2 | 3 | 4 |
| 5 | 6 | 7 | 8 |
| 9 | 10 | 11 | 12 |

FREE ZONE

ENTREPRENEURIAL GROWTH

FRONTIER

GLOBAL

- - - - - - - - - - -

INDUSTRY

- - - - - - - - - - -

MARKET

- - - - - - - - - - -

COMPANY

- - - - - - - - - - -

TEAMWORK

- - - - - - - - - - -

PERSONAL

# Total Cash Confidence Scorecard

Turn the page to view the Mindset Scorecard and read through the four statements for each mindset. Give yourself a score of 1 to 12 based on where your own mindset falls on the spectrum. Put each mindset's score in the first column at the right, and then add up all eight and put the total at the bottom.

Then, think about what scores would represent progress for you over the next quarter. Write these in the second scoring column, add them up, and write in the total.

When you compare the two scores, you can see where you want to go in terms of your achievements and ambitions.

| Mindsets | 1 | 2 | 3 | 4 | 5 | 6 |
|---|---|---|---|---|---|---|
| **1** **Your Value-Creating KASH** | You are clueless about how moneymaking is achieved, so much so that you feel those who do know how to achieve it have an unfair advantage. | | | You know that the most successful moneymaking achievers don't follow conventional rules, and now you want to know how they do it. | | |
| **2** **Always Bigger, Better Bypass** | You are always totally outside of other people's moneymaking systems, feeling confused and isolated while they make progress. | | | You're frustrated and tired of trying to fit into the lower ranks of other moneymaking approaches, and now you want to bypass them. | | |
| **3** **Continually Improving Value** | Your anger and resentment about having no ability to make money of your own prevents you from doing anything that's valuable to others. | | | You are resolutely committed to not selling the same commodities everybody else sells, and are going to try something new. | | |
| **4** **Right Place, Right Timing** | Your lack of daily value creation in all situations means that there's never any good opportunity for you to be a successful moneymaker. | | | You're increasingly aware that your money frustrations are due to your failure to consciously focus on creating timely value for others. | | |
| **5** **Predictably Expansive** | You are permanently caught in an endless cycle of never having enough money, which means that bad surprises are what you expect. | | | You know for certain that your moneymaking capability will never increase until you courageously commit to creating bigger value. | | |
| **6** **Profitably Accelerating Teamwork** | You are increasingly surrounded by others who create little or no value in their daily lives and who also lack moneymaking capabilities. | | | You have no interest in the conventional formula of long, hard, boring work and now you're looking for a multiplier solution. | | |
| **7** **Always More Useful** | You've never learned how to be successful in any area of your life, and so you never have a structure today to improve tomorrow. | | | You're starting to realize more and more that learning from your own trial and error is the only way to customize your future. | | |
| **8** **Can't Do It Wrong** | Your lifelong failure to make money means that you'll never understand how to approach any future situation by first creating value. | | | You've continually learned from your mistakes and failures to the point where avoiding them is becoming more predictable. | | |
| **Scorecard** | → → → → | | | → → → → | | |

| 7 | 8 | 9 | 10 | 11 | 12 | Score Now | Score Next |
|---|---|---|---|---|---|---|---|
| You've always obeyed the conventional rules for earning, saving, and investing, and have no respect for those who have failed. | | | You always focus on integrating your own unique Knowledge, Attitudes, Skills, and Habits into value creation that produces more money. | | | | |
| You feel safe and secure by being associated with and supported by moneymaking systems of far smarter people. | | | Your unique KASH formula always enables you to create bigger and better revenue and profit results from year to year. | | | | |
| You have always made your money by selling existing products and services that "experts" have told you are always moneymakers. | | | Your confidence about growing your financial results enables you to focus on improving the value you create for your clientele. | | | | |
| You make sure that your ability to make and keep money enables you to maintain your present level of conventional status going forward. | | | Your greater focus on creating unique value — superior to any competitors — enables you to always be ready for the next best opportunity. | | | | |
| You always play it safe with your money, never risking what you've already saved and invested for anything new and exciting. | | | Your improved alertness and responsiveness always make each year's greater money-making a sure thing. | | | | |
| Your single professional goal during the years when you are making predictable money is to have secure savings after you retire. | | | Your predictable cash-growing system enables you to continually attract individuals whose superior teamwork skills free you up. | | | | |
| Your whole approach to the future is based on conforming to the consensus of what more successful people have told you to do. | | | You notice as you increasingly grow — while commoditized competitors slow, stop, and fail — that you have a secret formula that works. | | | | |
| You've only ever created value according to the rules and skills that others taught you, and so far that's always been good enough. | | | You and your team have improved and expanded your value creation so consistently that it's practically impossible to get anything wrong. | | | | |
| ➡ ➡ ➡ ➡ | | | ➡ ➡ ➡ ➡ | | | | |

## About The Author
# Dan Sullivan

 Dan Sullivan is the founder and president of The Strategic Coach Inc. and creator of The Strategic Coach® Program, which helps accomplished entrepreneurs reach new heights of success and happiness. He has over 40 years of experience as a strategic planner and coach to entrepreneurial individuals and groups. He is author of over 30 publications, including *The 80% Approach*™, *The Dan Sullivan Question*, *Ambition Scorecard*, *Wanting What You Want*, *The 4 C's Formula*, *The 25-Year Framework*, *The Game Changer*, *The 10x Mind Expander*, *The Mindset Scorecard*, *The Self-Managing Company*, *Procrastination Priority*, *The Gap And The Gain*, *The ABC Breakthrough*, *Extraordinary Impact Filter*, *Capableism*, *My Plan For Living To 156*, *WhoNotHow*, *Your Life As A Strategy Circle*, *Who Do You Want To Be A Hero To?*, *Free Zone Frontier*, *Always Be The Buyer*, and *Simplifier-Multiplier Collaboration*, and is co-author with Catherine Nomura of *The Laws of Lifetime Growth*.

Made in the USA
Middletown, DE
29 June 2021